FIRE & WATER

BOOK OF ELEMENTS

SUNBIRD
PENGUIN

Published by Ladybird Books Ltd 2013
A Penguin Company
Penguin Books Ltd, 80 Strand, London, WC2R 0RL, UK
Penguin Group (USA) Inc., 375 Hudson Street, New York 10014, USA
Penguin Books Australia Ltd, 707 Collins Street, Melbourne, Victoria 3008, Australia
 (A division of Pearson Australia Group Pty Ltd)
Canada, India, New Zealand, South Africa

Written by Barry Hutchison
Sunbird is a trademark of Ladybird Books Ltd

www.ladybird.com

ISBN: 978-1-40939-144-9
002
Printed in China

ALWAYS LEARNING   PEARSON

FIRE & WATER

BOOK OF ELEMENTS

CONTENTS

FIRE

WATER

WELCOME!
FROM FLYNN AND HUGO

Welcome aboard, Flynn fans! It's time for
me to tell you all you'll ever need to
know about Fire and Water. They're two of
the most powerful Elements in all of Skylands.
In fact, they're almost as awesome as I
am. Ha ha! (Just kidding, they're not
even close!)

Well, Flynn is right about one thing (there's a first time for everything, I suppose) - Fire and Water are indeed two of the most powerful Elements in Skylands. I've compiled some fascinating information on each of them, which you will find on the pages that follow. Happy learning!

WHERE DOES FIRE COME FROM?

I once asked Flynn what he knew about Fire and he said: "It's hot." And he has the nerve to call himself an expert . . .

Fire is one of the most ancient sources of power in all of Skylands. My research suggests Fire is so old that it existed even before our written records began (which isn't very helpful, I must admit). Today, much of our landscape is swollen with fiery, belching volcanoes. More importantly, it's one of the eight Elements that, long ago, were brought together to form the Core of Light.

Being the brightest of the Elements, Fire plays an important role in helping to keep the Darkness at bay. Skylanders powered by the Fire Element, such as Flameslinger and Eruptor, have proven highly effective in defending Skylands from the evil Kaos.

WHEN IT COMES TO BATTLING EVIL FORCES, THERE'S NO POWER QUITE LIKE FIRE POWER!

FIERY BEASTS

Until recently, lava creatures lurked deep beneath the surface of Skylands. No one even knew they existed until, one fateful night, the hot-tempered beasts had an argument that quickly led to a full-scale riot. Friends battled friends, family fought family, and strangers put fireworks beneath the bottoms of other strangers, then ran away laughing.

LAVA LIFE CAN BE HOT, HOT, HOT!

The battle became so heated and the pressure so great, that their home literally popped open. Lava creatures (including our very own Eruptor) were fired out like flaming cannonballs and scattered all across Skylands.

LIFE IN LAVA LAKES

As its name suggests, Lava Lakes was a rather hot place. Most of the time, its inhabitants enjoyed the blistering heat, but occasionally it would become unbearable even for them. When this happened, tempers would flare. During such periods, even small family disagreements could last for several weeks, and would usually end with at least one family member exploding noisily.

Some of the angrier locals tried to control their tempers using meditation – but this did not go well. Of the eleven who tried, five were blown up, three spontaneously combusted, two melted and one turned into a very small flame imp. No one has been able to figure out why this last one happened, least of all the flame imp himself.

When their home erupted it wasn't just the lava creatures who popped out. Many artefacts were launched into the world above, too. Turn the page to see a singed extract from a Lava Lakes holiday brochure that also survived . . .

YOUR HOLIDAY IN ...
LAVA LAKES!

Looking to get away from it all? To escape to somewhere warm? Perhaps you're after that perfect tan? Then Lava Lakes is the ideal holiday destination for you!

Ahead of your break in Lava Lakes, here are some things you might want to pack:

Protective clothing

Temperatures in Lava Lakes can reach up to 1,200°C! Be sure to come prepared with a lead-lined suit and a diamond hat. Sandals are not recommended.

Water

Because of the blistering heat, water is in short supply. There's none, actually, so bring plenty. Unfortunately it will evaporate almost immediately, so be sure to drink it quickly!

Sporting Activites

Here in Lava Lakes we just love competitive sports! Here are a few you might like to try during your visit:

1. **Heady Flameball**
2. **Blazing Trousers**
3. **Hop-scorch**
4. **Ooyah, Me Head's On Fire!**
5. **Pin the Molten Rock to the Other Bit of Molten Rock**

We can't wait to see you! And remember, whatever you choose to do in Lava Lakes, we guarantee you'll have a sweltering good time!*

*This is probably not true.

HOT HEAD

DID YOU KNOW?

The Giant Hot Head was the first ever Skylander to come across magical oil. Unfortunately, he then decided to take a bath in it, resulting in a gigantic explosion. It was during this cataclysmic blast that he is believed to have first uttered his catchphrase "Hey! I'm on fire!" . . . although rumours suggest the original version was: "Aaaargh, help! Someone find a hose, quick!"

FACTFILE

- Giant in stature, short in temper
- Can generate a never-ending supply of fuel
- Appropriately named for a Skylander whose skull is constantly ablaze
- Handy clawed fingers and toes

FIRE RATING

100

HOT DOG

FACTFILE

- Likes burying things – especially imps
- Once burned his nose when attempting to chase his own tail
- Born in the fiery belly of the Popcorn Volcano
- Fiercely loyal to his friends

DID YOU KNOW?

Hot Dog has an incredible sense of smell. His highly-sensitive nostrils can sniff out trouble from miles away, and detect a guff from the next town over. After helping the Skylanders on an early mission, the fire pup was invited back to Master Eon's Citadel - where he showed his appreciation by burying the wise old Portal Master's favourite staff.

74%

FIRE RATING

IGNITOR

FACTFILE

- Not a big fan of witches
- Fights evil with the fiery blade of his flaming sword
- Slayed the Red Dragon after a scorching battle
- Trapped inside his cursed armour (which makes going to the toilet difficult)

DID YOU KNOW?

When Ignitor isn't defending Skylands or hunting for the witch who tricked him into wearing his cursed armour, he finds other ways to put his flaming sword to use. As well as being a devastating weapon in the fight against evil, it's also great for toasting marshmallows on.

67%

FIRE RATING

SUNBURN

FACTFILE

- Half dragon, half phoenix
- Loves playing pranks
- Hatched from an egg in the heart of a volcano
- Flamethrower breath turns up the heat on his enemies

DID YOU KNOW?

Sunburn has the ability to teleport, which comes in very handy when playing pranks on his fellow Skylanders. He finds it highly amusing to appear right behind Eruptor, shout "boo!", and then teleport away again. Eruptor, it must be said, usually fails to see the funny side.

FIRE RATING

66%

FLAMESLINGER

FACTFILE

- Once saved the life of a drowning fire spirit
- Blindfolds himself to hide the strange fire burning in his eyes
- Enchanted fire boots grant him lightning-fast speed
- His "second sight" allows him to see far-off places and events

DID YOU KNOW?

Flameslinger's enchanted fire boots may give him super-speed, but they also ruin every carpet he sets foot on. This is why Flameslinger is rarely invited round to anyone's house for dinner.

FIRE RATING

70%

ERUPTOR

71%

FIRE RATING

FACTFILE

- Hails from a fiery realm that unexpectedly exploded

- Hates being in big crowds. Or small crowds. Or any crowds, for that matter

- The ultimate hot head (apart from Hot Head himself, obviously), with a fiery temper and a very short fuse

- Doesn't need oven gloves when helping in the kitchen

DID YOU KNOW?

Eruptor's temper can erupt at the slightest thing. When he isn't getting angry at the forces of Kaos, he's blowing a fuse about smaller things. Anything from creaky floorboards to people not covering their mouths when they cough can make him literally explode with rage.

FIRE

ire is the most unpredictable of the Elements. A
flickering candle can transform into a raging inferno
if not watched carefully. Fire is dangerous, and yet also
strangely hypnotic.

And hot! Don't forget hot!
Yes, thank you, Flynn. I'm well aware that Fire is hot.
No problem.
Stop interrupting! Sorry. Where was I? Oh yes. Because of its
raw power and hypnotic qualities, Fire is employed by both the
forces of good, and the agents of evil . . .

LAVA KINGS

ith their
flamethrower arms
and habit of vomiting
flame imps everywhere,
these lumbering, burning
brutes demonstrate just
how scary Fire can be
in the wrong hands. Of
course, strictly speaking,
they don't actually have
hands, but you know
what I mean.

IF YOU SEE A
LAVA KING,
LOOK BUT
DON'T TOUCH!

THE CORE OF LIGHT

Fire is one of the crucial components of the Core of Light, along with the seven other known Elements. The Core keeps us all safe by preventing the Darkness from dominating our world . . . which is probably why Kaos doesn't seem to like it very much.

WHAT SHALL WE DO WITH A ROTTING ROBBIE?

These zombies are slow-moving, dim-witted and leave a nasty whiff in their wake. What sets them apart from other nasties is that they can only be harmed by Fire attacks. Well, that or being shot in the face by a cannonball, but that would put anyone off their stride. If you ever find yourself surrounded by shuffling Rotting Robbies, you'd better hope a Fire Skylander arrives to turn up the heat!

MINING IS THE KEY

Ignitor is one tough cookie. Cali knows it takes more than strength to be a hero, though, so she set Ignitor a Heroic Challenge that would test more than just his might! She sent him to some dark underground caves to find some hidden treasure. Think that sounds easy? You don't know my Cali!

The paths through the caves were blocked by locked doors. Ignitor had to smash rocks until he found the keys. Oh, and did I mention the whole place was crawling with angry rhu-barbs? My Cali really knows how to help Skylanders unlock their full potential! See what I did there?

ISLE OF THE AUTOMATONS

Eruptor's temper is legendary, and he put it to good use when Cali sent him to a tropical island almost as beautiful as she is. The place was overrun by a whole range of nasties – not to mention a few huge, nearly-indestructible robots! Eruptor burned and melted his way through in no time – and, when it comes to blowing up big robots, he is the bomb! The island is now the perfect place for a picnic! As long as you don't mind all the lava and molten metal that Eruptor left behind, that is.

ERUPTOR SURE KNOWS HOW TO MAKE AN ENTRANCE!

IN THE BAG

FLYNN'S FABLES

Before Master Eon made him a Skylander, Sunburn – like me – was a bit of a celebrity superstar in his own right. Everyone wanted a piece of that guy. Literally! One time, back when he was younger and not quite so battle-hardened, someone came very close to trapping him.

Years before he was even born, people were talking about Sunburn. The legend of the half-dragon, half-phoenix was discussed constantly by soothsayers, psychics and people with nothing better to do with their time. Everyone got very excited when he eventually exploded from his volcano egg. As soon as poor baby Sunburn hatched, hunters, witch-doctors and treasure-seekers all started to come after him.

The feathers from a phoenix-dragon (Phoegon? Dragnix? Who knows?) are supposed to have the magical ability to cure . . . something. Dandruff, maybe? I forget. Anyway, everyone wanted those feathers, and that meant

he discovered his fiery breath couldn't burn through the sack he almost started to worry.

Almost. You see, the hunter had failed to realize one very important fact: Sunburn has the ability to teleport. Before the hunter could say, "I'm going to be rich beyond my wildest dreams!", Sunburn popped up right next to him. And it wasn't a happy Sunburn, either. The hunter was last seen running for the hills with his hair on fire, and Sunburn has never allowed himself to be captured again since. Way to go, little Phoegon! Or Dragnix! Or whatever you are!

capturing Sunburn!

Sunburn was usually able to avoid capture pretty easily (it turns out hunters, witch-doctors and treasure-seekers aren't too smart). That is until one day, when Sunburn was having an afternoon snooze beside a lava pool. One sneaky hunter managed to slip a flameproof sack over Sunburn and quickly tie it shut! Poor Sunburn didn't know what was happening, and when

ELEMENTAL GATES:
FIRE LOCATIONS

Dotted across Skylands are a number of gates that only Fire Skylanders can open. After months of research, investigation and one rather lucky guess, I have managed to pinpoint the location of some of these gates.

GOO FACTORY

Some gates are easier to reach than others. The gate at the Goo Factory is simple. When you enter the factory, turn left and there it is. A tricky block-pushing puzzle awaits.

ACCESS OF LOCATION

HARD

EASY

TROLL WAREHOUSE

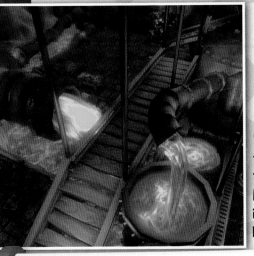

Another Fire Gate can be found at the end of the access catwalks in the Troll Warehouse. You'll have to fight your way there, then battle flame imps and lava kings on the other side.

ACCESS OF LOCATION

HARD

EASY

LAVA LAGOON

This gate, at Lava Lakes Railway, is well protected. Drow spearmen and a spell punk will try to prohibit your entry. Defeat them to gain access.

ACCESS OF LOCATION

HARD

EASY

DROPPING IN ON KAOS

FLYNN'S FABLES

Did I ever tell you about the time me and my balloon saved the whole of Skylands? No? Well, it's true. Oh, sure, Flameslinger helped a little I suppose, but if it wasn't for that balloon and my good handsome self, Skylands would now be under Kaos' control.

It was late last year. Or maybe the year before. It was definitely one year, anyway. I was floating over some cliffs in my balloon, admiring the view and expertly managing not to crash by using all of my supremo skills.

Suddenly, who should I see down below but Kaos himself! I knew it was him right away. I'd recognize that big bald head anywhere. He had surrounded himself with minions and they were marching together in a big group, looking for trouble.

Obviously I would have jumped down and stopped them but . . . my leg got stuck in, um, a bucket. Yeah, that's it.

Had it not been for that bucket I'd have jumped down there, and fought them off.

Luckily, Flameslinger was standing in their path. I don't know if it was coincidence that he was there, or whether his crazy second sight thingy had warned him danger was coming, but the Flamester was there with bow and arrow at the ready.

Now, Flameslinger is one tough dude, but even he couldn't handle the whole crowd on his own, and Kaos knew that. So Kaos just kept on walking, doing that crazy laugh of his every step of the way.

I held my breath and watched as Flameslinger drew back a fiery arrow. He pointed it straight at Kaos . . . and then he moved so it was pointing right up into the sky! I heard the THWIP of the string, then felt a great heat passing my face. Next thing I knew my balloon exploded.

Kaos must have heard the pop,

because I definitely didn't start screaming. He looked up just in time to see me in my basket falling towards him. He managed to leap to safety just in the nick of time, and Flameslinger sent him running with a few more well-aimed arrows.

And that was the day me and my balloon saved Skylands! That reminds me – Flameslinger never did pay me back for those repairs . . .

FLAMESLINGER FASHION

Flameslinger is more than just an amazing archer. He's something of a fashion icon, too! Being a very practical Elf, Flameslinger's outfit is functional as well as stylish.

PONY TAIL

This keeps Flameslinger's hair out of his face, which could be distracting, and stops it getting tangled in the string of his bow, which could be painful. Luckily for me, this isn't something I'll ever have to worry about.

MAGIC FIRE BOOTS

Another gift from the fire spirit, these boots not only look impressive, they also grant Flameslinger incredible speed. On the downside, they make his feet smell all sweaty, but no one has the nerve to tell him.

BLINDFOLD

Flameslinger wears his flame-red blindfold because he grew sick of people staring at the strange, supernatural flames that have flickered behind his eyes since birth. He also wears it because hitting targets is just too easy otherwise, and he does enjoy a challenge.

ENCHANTED BOW

Also gifted to him by the fire spirit, Flameslinger's bow can shoot arrows of fire without catching alight itself. Which is handy, because no one wants to take aim at an enemy and accidentally burn their own hand off.

ARMOUR

A combination of leather and chain mail, the armour is light enough to allow Flameslinger to move quickly, but strong enough to deflect most attacks. Mind you, he never stands still long enough for anyone to hit him.

ERUPTOR'S BIG BET

FLYNN'S FABLES

Once, Trigger Happy bet Eruptor that he couldn't stay calm for a whole hour. If he managed, then Trigger Happy would give him a dozen gold coins. Eruptor wasn't interested in the gold, but he wanted to prove to Trigger Happy that he could control his temper. He agreed to the bet, and Trigger Happy set right to work trying to force Eruptor to – well, erupt.

First up he said Eruptor had a face like a melted boulder, but the big Fire Skylander just ignored him. Then Trigger Happy took things up a gear by saying Eruptor's Lava Lob attack was "weaker than a Molekin's eyesight". You could see the big guy was less than pleased about that, but he managed to keep his cool – just.

I think that took Trigger Happy by surprise, but he soon

I'm not surprising anyone when I say that Eruptor has a really hot temper. He's the angriest guy I've ever met. He's even angrier than Cali was after I accidentally knocked her into that pile of sheep poo last week (and wow, she was really angry!).

started to pile on the pressure again. He 'borrowed' some snow cones from Slam Bam and lobbed them at Eruptor's head. They melted straight away, covering him in icy cold water – but still the big dude didn't lose his rag!

Trigger Happy kept it up for the full hour, prodding at Eruptor, throwing things at him, calling him names – anything he could think of to get the big lava guy fired up. Through it all, though, Eruptor managed to stay calm.

When the sixty minutes were finally up, Eruptor grinned broadly and demanded the gold coins for winning the bet. Trigger Happy nodded sadly.

Then, when Eruptor's back was turned, he fired both guns and twelve gold coins hit Eruptor directly on his big red rear end!

That did it! Eruptor exploded with rage – and Trigger Happy ran off giggling. Eruptor may have won the bet, but there's no doubting that Trigger Happy got the last laugh that day!

KNIGHT TIMES

Before Ignitor managed to defeat the wicked red dragon that threatened his homeland, several other knights tried – and all failed miserably. In tribute to these brave souls, here are their stories . . .

SIR TURBERTUS THE KNACKERED

Sir Turbertus was not the largest knight in the kingdom, nor was he the most feared. However, he was the first to challenge the red dragon, which means he was either the bravest, or the most foolish.

Aware that the red dragon was larger than most other dragons, Sir Turbertus had a blacksmith forge him a sword several metres long. It took him three long, tiring weeks to drag the enormous blade to the dragon's lair, by which point he was too exhausted to lift it – making it easy for the dragon to incinerate him on sight.

SIR HEADLUN THE FEARLESS

Headlun claimed to be a veteran slayer of dragons. He offered to kill the red dragon in return for a substantial reward.

MEET THE FAMILY

Flame imps are more of a nuisance than a real threat, but in some parts of Skylands you could encounter their more powerful cousins – gnashers. Just like flame imps, gnashers appear to be made of living fire. Unlike flame imps, their fire burns blue. This means they are even hotter – and more dangerous – than standard flame imps. Find yourself surrounded by a gaggle of gnashers and you'd better hope you're wearing your fire-proof underwear, because things are about to get very hot for you.

FLAME IMP FACTFILE

- Annoying
- Small
- Annoying
- Hot
- Really very annoying indeed
- Fast
- Noisy
- Did I mention annoying?

37

ARMOUR ESCAPE

FLYNN'S FABLES

Everyone knows the story of how Ignitor got himself turned into flame and sealed inside that armour of his. His mother had always warned him not to trust witches. Of course, Ignitor tried everything he could to break the curse, and some of his methods were nearly as dangerous as the red dragon itself!

Once he had slain the dragon, Ignitor returned to the witch's home to try to convince her to put him back to normal. When he got to her cottage he found it empty and a note on the kitchen table that simply read: 'Listen to your mum in future'.

Ignitor talked with all the wizards and warlocks he could find, but none of them could free him from his curse. He asked lots of Skylanders to help him, too. Gill Grunt tried spraying him with a jet of water, Hex tried casting an Undead spell and Whirlwind summoned a mighty wind in an attempt to blow his flames out.

After that all failed, Hugo suggested trying to get him out of his armour first. And Drobot thought that some old Arkeyan Tech might do the job. So Ignitor lay under the tracks of an ancient battle tank, and Drobot managed to activate it long enough for it to roll right over Ignitor's back. Instead of breaking open the armour, though, it just pressed him into the ground. It took all four of Slam Bam's arms to pull him free, but Ignitor still hadn't given up. He's quite the trooper! He is a brave knight, after all.

Everyone had suggested ways of cracking the curse, but none

of them had worked. Ol' Ignitor was getting desperate.

But there was one person he hadn't asked for advice. His mum. He trudged to her house and asked her what he should do. She looked him up and down, then gave him a peck on the cheek and told him he looked just perfect the way he was.

Ignitor didn't try to change himself after that. I guess he finally realized that his mum really does know best!

FIRE:
ELEMENTS UNITE

Being the brightest and flamiest of all the Elements, Fire combines with the others in a number of unique ways.

WEAKNESS

Water is the natural enemy of Fire, and Fire Skylanders must be extra cautious when dealing with the Water Element or they may find their flames well and truly extinguished.

HOW FIRE ENTWINES WITH THE OTHER ELEMENTS

AIR
More oxygen means a bigger burn

EARTH
Scorches the Earth for added strength

LIFE
Warms the blood of all living things

MAGIC
Heats Magic to whole new levels

TECH
Welds the parts of incredible gadgets

UNDEAD
Provides smoky shadows for the Undead

WATER
Makes Skylands' water bubble and boil

FIRE
SKYLANDERS

SUNBURT

IGNITOR

ERUPTOR

FLAMESLINGER

HOT DOG

HOT HEAD

WATER
SKYLANDERS

CHILL

ZAP

WHAM-SHELL

GILL GRUNT

THUMPBACK

SLAM BAM

43

WHERE DOES WATER COME FROM?

Where does Water come from? The sky. What? You want more? Oh, very well then. Water is present in all living things. Without it, few of the other Elements would ever have come to exist. Water takes many forms – a calm lake, a torrential rainfall, a furious typhoon – and Water Elementals come in just as wide a range of shapes and sizes.

Vast areas of Skylands are covered in Water, and beneath the surface lie a whole host of undersea kingdoms. There are creatures living down there who haven't even found out that dry land exists, never mind set foot on it. From heroic protectors like the Gillmen to monstrous fish like the Leviathan, Water supports and teems with all manner of life.

SUNKEN SHIPS ARE AMONG THE MANY SECRETS HIDDEN BENEATH THE WATERS OF SKYLANDS.

THE KINGDOM OF GOOD KING ROLAND

Good King Roland is a Crab King whose underwater domain lay hidden for centuries. Previous rulers were happy to keep the place a secret, but Roland (the father of our very own Wham-Shell!) decided to make his kingdom's presence known to the land-dwellers.

Soon his subjects were trading with the rest of Skylands, sending precious pearls to the surface. In return they asked for: "Any food that's not fish. Even some ham sandwiches would do, we're not fussy." Thankfully, the land-dwellers were happy to oblige.

Today, divers, submariners and anyone who can hold their breath for a really long time go down to visit the kingdom. Upon arrival, they discover a beautiful place where the buildings are made of polished shell, the streets are paved with priceless gems and everyone munches delightedly on soggy ham sandwiches.

THE PALACE

Home of Good King Roland and his family, the palace was built from the upturned hull of a vast fishing boat that sunk several centuries ago. It is made up of a number of distinct areas, including 'The Throne Room' where Roland meets his subjects, 'The Ball Room' where Roland and his family play a variety of fast-paced team sports, and 'The Dead Fisherman Room' which is usually kept locked.

THE FISH RESTAURANT

Pop in and you can have your choice of big fish, small fish, long fish, stubby fish, fish with a bit of a weird face, fish with no face at all, two-headed fish, two-tailed fish, scaly fish, scary fish, hairy fish, sweary fish (with free ear plugs for the easily offended) and seventeen different types of eel, all of which taste exactly the same. The locals all got a bit sick of fish quite some time ago, which makes it easy to get a table.

SKYLANDS AQUATIC BESTIARY

The waters of Skylands are positively overflowing with life. From hopping crabs and tangled eels to bubble sharks and choir clams, there are more creatures down there than most land-dwelling types can even dream of. Here are just a few of them . . .

JUST LOOK AT THOSE TEETH!

THE LEVIATHAN

The Leviathan is an enormous shark-like monstrosity that inhabits Leviathan Lagoon (which is a bit of a coincidence). Think of the biggest thing you can imagine. Now double it. You're not even close to the size of the Leviathan. Unless you were originally thinking of the actual Leviathan itself, of course, in which case the actual Leviathan is now exactly half the size of the, um, imaginary double-sized Leviathan that you . . . that you . . . Look, the point I'm trying to make is: it's big.

TURTLES

The turtles in Skylands are no wimps, but they are used to being pushed around. Skylands turtles are too slow and lumbering to be able to fight Kaos, but they still do what they can to help defeat his dark forces. Usually, this involves being shoved in all directions by Skylanders, who use their shells as stepping stones to get to hard-to-reach places. They're quite happy having the likes of Eruptor and Stump Smash clumping all over their backs. At least, we assume they are. It's hard to tell from looking at them.

NAUTELOIDS

Nauteloids are nasty little crustaceans who can catch even the most alert Skylander unawares. They have a thick shell on their back to protect them, and a long saw-like nose with which to attack. Fortunately, dealing with a single nauteloid is not too difficult, as they can only attack in a straight line. Therefore, one of the best ways of dealing with a charging nauteloid is to stand in front of a brick wall, then step to one side just before it hits you. Bang goes one naughty nauteloid!

GILLMEN

There's something fishy about Gillmen - and that's their faces! And most of the rest of their bodies, come to think of it. Actually, if you think of a walking, talking fish, you're not far off. Many of them live on Oilspill Island, which is nicer than it sounds, although not much. They are famous across Skylands for their singing voices (although not in a good way). And of course for their military forces, which operate like a well-oiled machine.

THUMPBACK

100%

WATER RATING

DID YOU KNOW?

Despite being in cahoots with the pirates, Thumpback wasn't all that keen on skulduggery, and spent most of his days fishing instead. Once, when trying to reel in the fabled Leviathan Cloud Crab, he was pulled overboard and carried far away. This turned out to be an incredible stroke of luck, as soon afterwards the Phantom Tide was banished to the dreaded Chest of Exile.

FACTFILE

- Former pirate knave
- Sailed aboard the terrifying Phantom Tide
- It is rumoured that six fully grown Skylanders could fit inside his mouth. Not that they'd want to
- Has a passion for angling

CHILL

DID YOU KNOW?

As captain of the Queen's guard, Chill was once the most feared - and respected - of all the people in the Ice Kingdom. But when the Cyclops Army invaded, she could only watch as the Snow Queen was snatched away. Ashamed, Chill left the Ice Kingdom - and vowed never to return until she had tracked down her people's lost ruler.

WATER RATING

66%

FACTFILE

● Ex-personal guard of the Snow Queen

● Sworn enemy of the Cyclopses. Cyclopseses. Cyclopseseses. The one-eye people

● A proud, noble warrior - but not afraid to fight dirty

SLAM BAM

DID YOU KNOW?

Slam Bam's four arms allow him to put the squeeze on enemies, but they also grant him incredible juggling abilities. At one demonstration he was seen to juggle seventeen snowballs, three ice ogres and one very surprised Gill Grunt.

FACTFILE

- One of an ancient race of yetis
- Sculpts amazing ice statues
- Loves eating snow cones
- Expert ice surfer

WATER RATING

67%

ZAP

FACTFILE

- A water dragon who was raised by electric eels
- Has a real mischievous streak
- Loves to race, especially against dolphins
- Wears a golden harness powered by Elemental energy

71%

WATER RATING

DID YOU KNOW?

Zap was born into the High Water Dragon Royal Family. He would almost certainly have grown up to be king had a freak tide not carried him away from home. It is extremely difficult to keep a crown on underwater, though, so all things considered it was probably a lucky escape.

WHAM-SHELL

DID YOU KNOW?

Wham-Shell's razor-sharp teeth don't stay so perfectly white by themselves. He brushes them up to fourteen times a day with a toothbrush carved from coral, and toothpaste made from mashed fish scales.

FACTFILE

- Prince of a vast undersea realm
- Has a deep dislike of trolls
- Wields a magical mace
- His claws give more than just a nasty nip

WATER RATING

69%

GILL GRUNT

FACTFILE

- One of a race of Gillmen sworn to protect the seas
- A master with a harpoon gun
- His true love, a mermaid, was kidnapped by pirates
- Large, bulging eyes allow him to see well underwater

DID YOU KNOW?

Gill Grunt wasn't always as skilled with his jetpack as he is now. His first attempt at using it saw him launched screaming into the air like a rocket, where he collided with Spyro (who happened to be flying overhead). They both escaped unhurt, but even now Spyro jokes about the day Gill Grunt shot him down.

72%

WATER RATING

55

SECRETS OF THE ELEMENTS:
WATER

Water holds many secrets, and not just its hidden undersea cities. My research indicates that Water may have played a part in powering ancient Arkeyan technology . . .

CHARGING ARKEYAN TECH

The ancient Arkeyans were masters of Tech, and built huge war machines that they used to rule Skylands. Flynn informs me that, while these machines required Magic in order to work, they also needed something even more important: batteries. He claims the Arkeyans discovered that, if they trapped enough electric eels in jars, they could harness the electrical energy to power their contraptions.

This, of course, is nonsense. Never listen to Flynn.

WATER GATES

Upon activation, a Water Elemental gate becomes a swirling whirlpool, which drags the Skylander inside.

FRIGHTBEARD'S RETURN

One of Skylands' biggest mysteries surrounds the murky past of Captain Frightbeard. The giant sky pirate's terrifying ship, the Phantom Tide, is capable of gobbling up entire islands, even after a satisfying breakfast. Once banished to the Chest of Exile, he refuses to discuss how he ended up back at the helm of his massive vessel (and few are brave enough to ask him).

However, many believe he struck a deal for his freedom with an evil sorcerer. What was his side of the bargain? Whatever it was, he came out of the experience with one eye and several teeth fewer than he had at the beginning.

CALI'S HEROIC CHALLENGES

When she's not thinking about me, Cali is putting the Skylanders through some pretty gruelling training. Of course, I could do this kinda thing in my sleep. That's why she never asks me to complete a challenge . . . too easy!
Let's check some of them out . . .

JAILBREAK!

When Cali (whose eyes are perfect, by the way) set Gill Grunt a challenge to free some kidnapped Mabu, he got a close-up view of some peepers even freakier than his own. The Mabu had been captured by cyclopses – one-eyed brutes who like to eat poor Mabu for lunch! The cyclopses' stomachs were rumbling, and Gill Grunt had only a few minutes to free the Mabu from their cages. Luckily, he brought his harpoon and was able to see the monsters off. Those cyclopses didn't get a look in.

BREAK THE CATS

Ten ancient spirits had somehow become trapped inside some cat statues. How did they get there? Who knows? Who cares? But Zap was given the task of smashing the statues and freeing the spirits. Unfortunately for Zap, the statues were surrounded by Cali's vase collection, and that little water dragon was given strict orders not to damage any of them. I've got no idea why Cali needs a thousand identical vases, or why she leaves them scattered around a tropical island, but if that's what she wants then it's OK by me! Zap broke the statues and freed the spirits, and not a single vase was harmed.

WHO SAYS WATER AND ELECTRICITY DON'T MIX?

FLYNN'S FABLES

ARMED
AND
DANGEROUS

Did I ever tell you about the time Slam Bam saved Skylands with three arms behind his back? Sounds incredible, right? Well, I'm an incredible guy! And so is Slam Bam, I suppose.

Slam Bam was sitting by a lake waiting for Double Trouble to join him for sparring practice. He was chowing down on a snow cone or twelve, when he saw a whole army of trolls, chompies and other minions marching towards him. Leading the pack was the Evil Ice Yeti – a clone of Slam Bam that Kaos created with dark Magic.

Now, Slam Bam could probably have fought back most of the army, but his evil double was a match for him in almost every way. There was no way he could fight them all off by himself, and Double Trouble

was still nowhere to be seen.

Slam Bam had to think fast. Luckily, the big guy's not as dumb as he looks. He stepped in front of the army and issued a challenge to his evil clone. He challenged him to an arm-wrestling competition, to decide once and for all which of them was the strongest.

Now, the Evil Ice Yeti is as dumb as he looks, so he accepted. The yetis found a big flat rock and knelt down on either side of it, as the rest of the army gathered round to cheer their leader on.

Each yeti put three hands behind his back. They clasped hands, locked their wrists, and began to push. Slam Bam knew he wasn't going to win, but he knew he wasn't going to lose either. The yetis were exactly as strong as one another, which meant it could only be a draw. They were still pushing, and the crowd still cheering, when Double Trouble finally showed up.

The Evil Ice Yeti realized he'd been tricked, but it was too late. With Double Trouble as back-up, Slam Bam fought the army back, and Skylands was safe again – for a little while, at least.

ELEMENTAL GATES: WATER LOCATIONS

Just as Fire Skylanders have gates only they can pass through, so too do those powered by the Water Element. Many late nights spent pouring over maps and scrolls have led to the discovery of the gates listed below.

CHOMPIE PIT

WARNING: THESE CHOMPIES BITE (IN FACT, THEY DO VERY LITTLE ELSE).

There's a Water gate in the Chompie Pit area of Shattered Island. Look out for Blobbers - he'll be only too happy to point the gate out to you if you can't spot it yourself. Good old Blobbers.

DIFFICULTY

EASY ⬤⬤⬤⬤⬤ HARD

LEVIATHAN LAGOON

DIFFICULTY

HARD

EASY

When you first enter the lagoon, cross the water, but watch out for the hungry Leviathan lurking beneath! Just beyond the tiled bridge is a Water gate. A nasty thieving Hob 'n' Yaro will try to run off with the treasure on the other side. Long-range attack the little menace and claim the prize.

FAIRY RING

HARD

DIFFICULTY

EASY

In Perilous Pastures you'll find a turtle balancing at the edge of a cliff. Apologize in advance, then shove it off the edge. Follow it down and you'll find a Water gate leading to a diabolically difficult block puzzle.

MISSING MACE MYSTERY

FLYNN'S FABLES

Wham-Shell's mace has been in his family for generations. It's not just a weapon; it's an ancient piece of undersea royal history. So you can imagine how stressed out he was when he lost it.

I first heard about the missing mace when Wham-Shell grabbed hold of me and demanded to know if I'd taken it. Under normal circumstances I'd have karate chopped him for yanking my arm like that, but I could see the poor guy was upset so I let it go.

Wham-Shell's usually a pretty together kind of guy, but that day he was furious. I hadn't seen him so angry since the time he stumbled upon that oil rig full of trolls. That mace sure got put to good use that day, let me tell you!

Anyway, I agreed to use my incredible tracking skills to help look for the weapon, and the two of us set off to find it. We searched everywhere – in crates and barrels, up trees – but we just could not see it anywhere.

Wham-Shell was starting to

get really worried. That mace is a priceless heirloom and he was worried what his dad was going to say if he couldn't find it.

I got him to think back to the last place he'd seen it. He was thinking about this when a ball bounced off the back of his shell. A little Mabu came running after the ball, and when he saw Wham-Shell he went a funny pale colour, then turned and ran off.

We chased after him and found Blobbers and some other Mabu playing a game of blatter ball,

using Wham-Shell's mace as the bat! Everyone froze, expecting Wham-Shell to lose his temper, but Whammy was so pleased to see his mace that he joined in the game!

Now, whenever he isn't using it to fight the Darkness, Wham-Shell joins in the blatter ball fun – although he stops just short of using precious family antiques as equipment.

HUGO'S NOTES

PIRATE PERIL

The one downside of water is that it tends to become a home for lowdown, good-for-nothing, shabby-bearded pirates. The waters of Skylands are full of them — from tiny grub pirates (who mainly steal hair and ideas) to huge whale pirates who would swallow entire shiploads of loot, if only they could be bothered to drag their gigantic bellies around in pursuit.

ARRRF

PIRATE FACTFILE

- Pirates of Skylands can be found not only in the water, but also in the sky. It is SKYlands, after all.
- Pirate beards are so dense that they can be used to store a prawn lunch for several weeks before it begins to go off.
- Pirates spend so much time stealing from each other that, on long voyages, they often end up with exactly the same possessions that they started off with.
- The biggest pirate booty ever recorded included 6,004 jewels, twenty-three gems, an entire wardrobe of gold-lined trousers and a fish-trumpet.

SEA SHANTIES

When they're not gambling, pillaging and making the murky depths even murkier by dangling their stinking tootsies overboard, pirates like to sing. Here are two examples of their favourite sing-along shanties:

BEING A PIRATE IS A RIGHT OLD LAUGH

Now back in days of olden times,
When waters were still young,
We'd steal the knees of a trollverine,
And lie back in the sun,
We'd paint our elbows tangerine,
And when all that was done,
We'd tie our mast to a merman's chin,
And have our pirate fun!

PIRATE RECRUITMENT SONG
(SUNG IN KEY OF "ARRR!")

Yo ho ho and a squiddler's face,
Come join our pirate throng,
We've sailed across the Skylands sky,
And sung our pirate song,
We'll hide your treasure in our pants,
And do all that is wrong,
Like painting rude bits on our sails,
And letting off a pong.

ZAP-TASTIC PRANK

FLYNN'S FABLES

My little water dragon buddy, Zap, has always loved practical jokes. He's got a nose for mischief, and one time he even managed to catch me out. Hard to believe I know!

I had taken my Cali on a picnic high on a hilltop. It was a glorious day – the sun was shining, the grass was green and I was even more witty and entertaining than I usually am. The picnic was a real joint effort – Cali had spent hours making some amazing food, and I had brought the plates. Well, technically just one plate. I'd sort of expected her to bring her own. Still, she said she didn't mind eating off her lap, so it was fine.

Anyway, things were going very smoothly. The sun was behind me, which always makes me look smouldering and mysterious. Cali was squinting at me when she suddenly looked over my shoulder and gasped.

I turned around and saw a huge hairy beast come bounding up the hillside towards us. It ran on four stubby legs which I could only just see beneath a mass of long white hair. The hair stood straight out, so it looked like a big spiky ball with feet.

Three more of the creatures came hopping up around us. Someone let out a high-pitched scream. It may have been Cali, or it may have been me, I'm not sure. Probably Cali, but please don't tell her I said that.

I started running for my balloon, scattering sandwiches and cakes everywhere. I was just jumping in the basket when one of the monsters spoke. It said, "Baaaa".

Suddenly Zap appeared, and he and Cali started laughing. It turns out that electricity makes sheep's wool stand on end. What I thought were big spiky scary monsters were actually just sheep. Cali and Zap had planned the whole joke from the start.

Of course, I knew all along that it was a practical joke, but I didn't want to hurt their feelings so I pretended to be terrified. Uh, yes, pretended. That's right. Just pretended.

GILL'S MERMAID QUEST

Merfolk aren't always easy to get along with. They spend hours gazing at their own reflections in shimmering surfaces, they're constantly practising holding their breath, and they become grumpy when their skin gets dry.

Despite these obstacles, Gill Grunt managed to find one who instantly became his true love. The pair spent a brief but happy period skimming stones, singing songs and gazing into each other's gigantic gogglesome eyes. But alas, their romance came to an abrupt end when his mer-love was mer-napped by pesky pirates.

Gill vowed to track down his scaly siren, and searches the seas (and skies) for her to this very day. But Skylands is vast, and Gill Grunt is quite short. Finding his true love is like trying to find a needle in a haystack, only the haystack is thousands of kilometres wide and the needle is always moving. And guarded by angry pirates.

Still, some nights when the lagoons are still, Gill swears he can hear her voice drifting across the water, singing of their lost love. This would be deeply romantic if she could sing, but unfortunately she has a voice like a bubble shark choking on seaweed.

MER-JOKES

Q. Why did the mermaid look the other way?
A. Because the seaweed.

Q. What part of a merman weighs the most?
A. The scales.

Q. Why do mermaids never share?
A. They're too shellfish.

Q. Why was the mermaid embarrassed?
A. Because she saw the ship's bottom.

MOTHER-IN-LAW MER-RESCUE

For many years the sailors of Skylands did their best to avoid merpeople, because an old legend warned that mermaids liked nothing more than luring unsuspecting crewmen to their deaths. Also, they're a bit weird looking, and sailors aren't generally keen on weird-looking things.

All that changed, however, when the captain of a trading ship accidentally knocked his seventy-year-old mother-in-law overboard while showing her how to scrub the poopdeck. The poor woman would almost certainly have drowned, had she not been rescued by a passing mermaid. The captain was said to be "sobbing with joy" when his mother-in-law was returned safe and well, and since that day mermaids have been looked on much more favourably.

GILL'S PORTRAIT OF HIS TRUE LOVE.

IT'S THE PITS

FLYNN'S FABLES

Before Gill Grunt was a Skylander he was a soldier in the Gillmen Marines. Gillmen Marines are some of the toughest troopers who have ever lived. These guys eat megasharks for breakfast, nauteloids for lunch, and then maybe a light salad for dinner, because there's no point in overdoing things.

Gill, being a close personal friend of mine, once told me a story about how his whole platoon was almost wiped out by a nest of pit spiders. They had been sent on a training exercise in the middle of the night. The mission: to cross a desert, retrieve a flag and bring it back to HQ before the sun came up. Now, the thing about Gillmen is they love the wet and hate the dry, so they were in a hurry to get the flag and get back home for a dip in the pool. In fact, they were in so much of a hurry that they didn't notice the huge spider's web on the ground. Big mistake!

The web was actually covering a deep hole. The whole platoon fell down the pit – all except Gill Grunt, who had stopped to write his girlfriend's name in the sand. When he heard the shouts of the rest of his squad, he ran to see what the problem was, and only just avoided falling down the pit himself.

He peered over the edge and saw a terrible sight. His squad was surrounded by five massive pit spiders. Now, I know you've never met a pit spider before. How do I know? Because you're still alive!

The marines had dropped their weapons in the fall, leaving them defenceless. Thinking fast, Gill blasted the sides of the pit with his water cannon, turning the sand into sticky mud. The marines down below hurled handfuls of mud at the spiders' eyes, blinding them big-time! Double-G then tossed down a length of web and pulled his friends to safety one by one.

So next time Gill Grunt is boring you with stories of his lost girlfriend, don't tell him to shut up. Your life might just depend on it!

SLAM BAM'S SNOW CONES

There's an old joke in Skylands:

Q. What does a yeti eat for dinner?

A. Anything it wants.

Most of the time this is probably true. If a yeti is hungry, nothing will stop it from eating whatever takes its fancy. Luckily for the other Skylanders, Slam Bam is not your typical yeti. When he gets hungry there is just one food he reaches for - snow cones. And he has been kind enough to share some of his favourite recipes with us . . .

FISH SURPRISE

Ingredients: Fish, ice

Method: Take your ice.
Add your fish.
Eat immediately.

Hugo's note: Slam Bam tells me it has 'surprise' in the name because the fish usually looks very surprised indeed.

HYDROSIUM CRUSH

Ingredients: Juice of one hydrosium plant, ice, antidote

Method: Take ice. Add hydrosium juice. Eat immediately. Consume antidote.

Hugo's note: There's nothing tastier than a hydrosium. It's just a pity that, when juiced, it becomes poisonous. Remember to take the antidote within four seconds of finishing, or your head will swell up and your legs will fall off.

THE CASTAWAY

Ingredients: Ice, more ice

Method: Take ice. Add ice. Eat immediately. Wish you weren't stuck on an iceberg with nothing else to eat.

Hugo's note: Slam Bam ate plenty of these back when he was stuck on a floating iceberg with nothing else to eat. Not the most exciting flavour, he tells me, but a very easy recipe to try out.

SHOCKTASTIC SUNDAE

Ingredients: Electric eels, ice, first aid kit

Method: Take two cups of ice. Insert electric eels, then cover with more ice and allow to refreeze. Eat immediately. Administer first aid.

Hugo's note: Be careful; this mouth-tingling treat may well make your tongue explode. In fact, it definitely will.

WATER:
ELEMENTS UNITE

Just like in Slam Bam's icy snow cones, Water is a key ingredient in the Core of Light, where it lends its power to the other Elements in a number of remarkable ways.

WEAKNESS

The Life element is strongest against Water. The grass, flowers and plants that are part of Life, suck Water through their roots to give them strength. Which is great for them, but not so handy for poor Water.

HOW WATER ENTWINES WITH THE OTHER ELEMENTS

AIR
Combines with Air to create powerful storms

EARTH
Turns dry, dusty Earth to slick, slippery mud

FIRE
Combines with Fire to help smoke out agents of Darkness

LIFE
Nourishes plants so Life can grow

MAGIC
Helps Magic to flow freely

TECH
Boosts Tech with a short, sharp shock

UNDEAD
Floods the Undead with ghostly strength

FAREWELL!

I know, I know - that's a whole lot of information to remember. Don't worry, it took years for me to cram all that knowledge into this handsome head of mine, and I'm smarter than most! Go back and read from the start a few times if you have to. It's nothing to be ashamed of. I'd pay close attention to my bits and skim past Hugo's, though. You've got to have your priorities right! Boom!

THE BATTLE
AGAINST KAOS
CONTINUES!

Yes, very funny, Flynn. Pay no attention, Portal Master. Flynn's tales may be more exciting, but half of them never happened, and the other half probably didn't either. Information, not barely-remembered fantasy, is the most effective weapon against Kaos. Although a really big sword is quite effective, too, if push comes to shove. Good luck, Portal Master, and be careful out there . . .